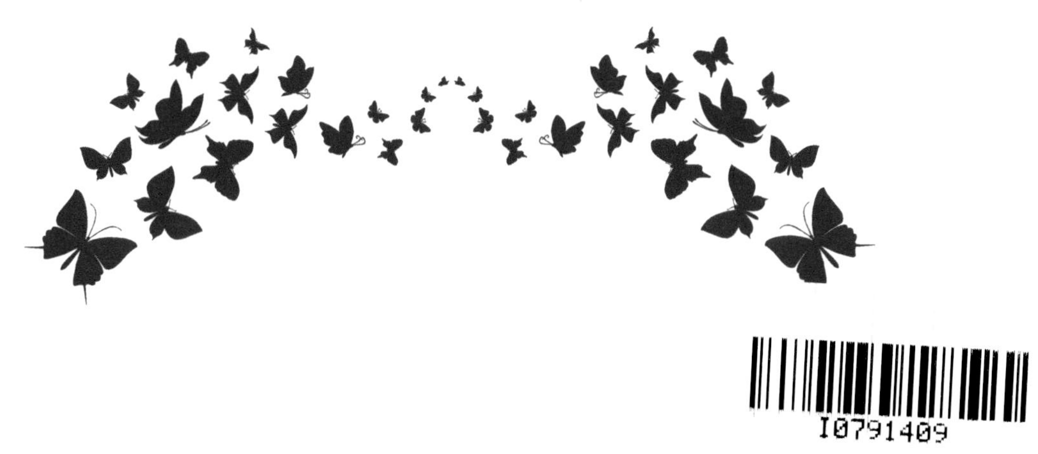

The picture book for

Butterfly

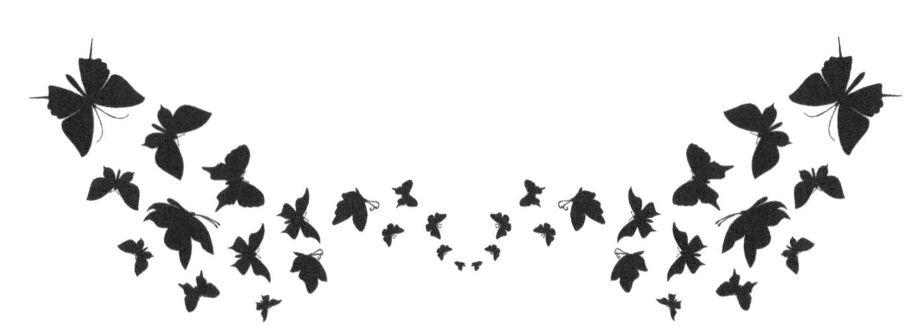

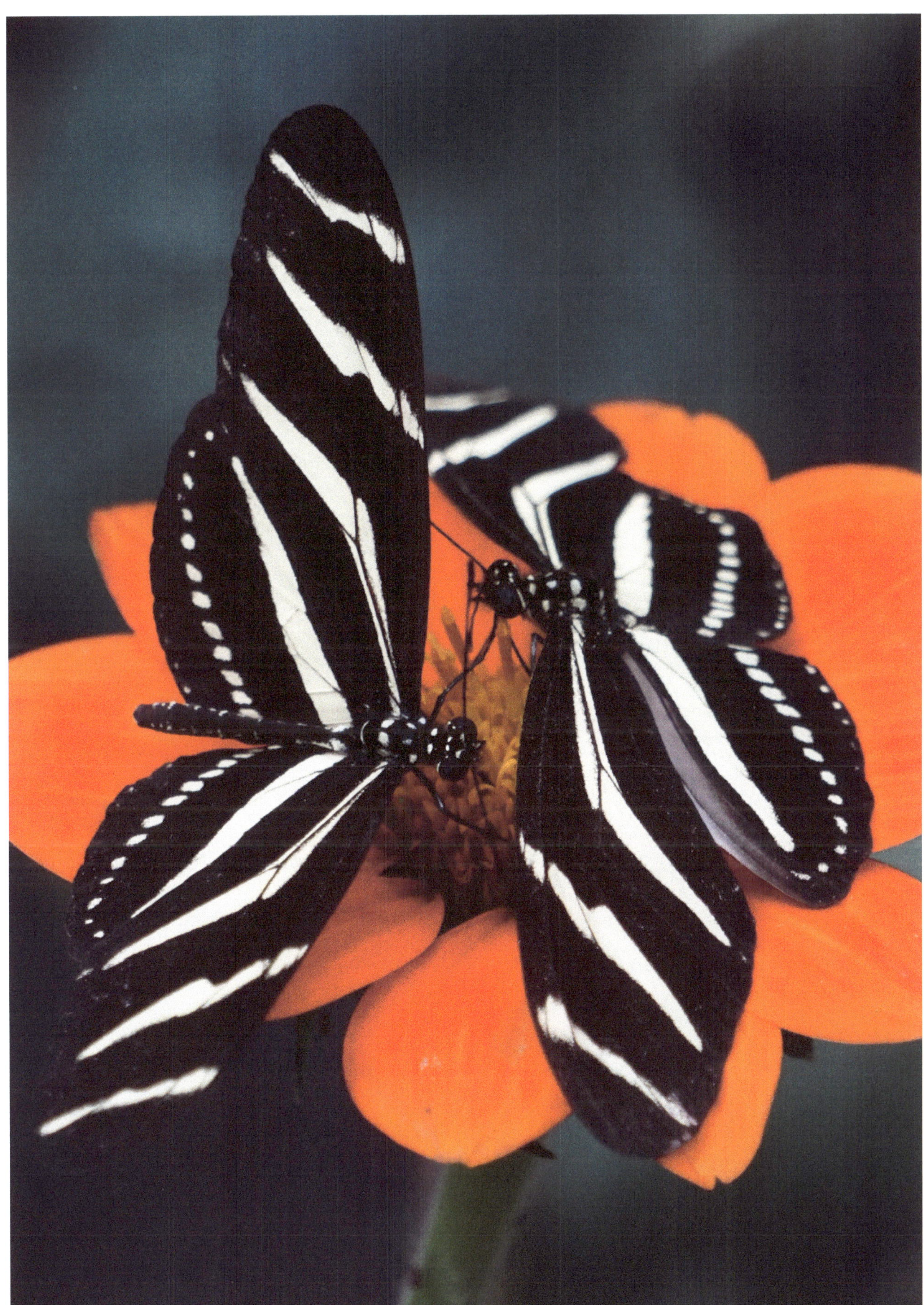

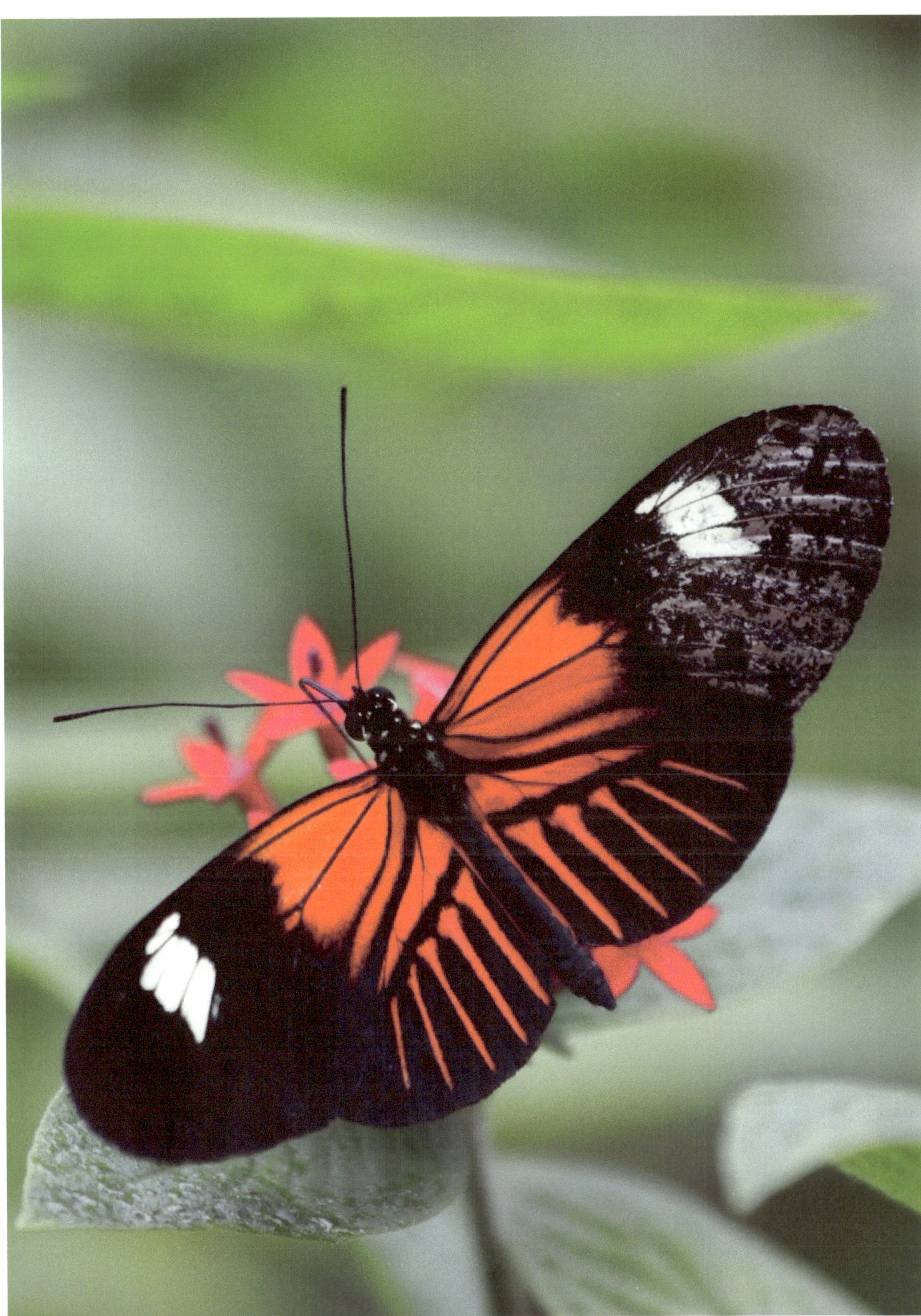

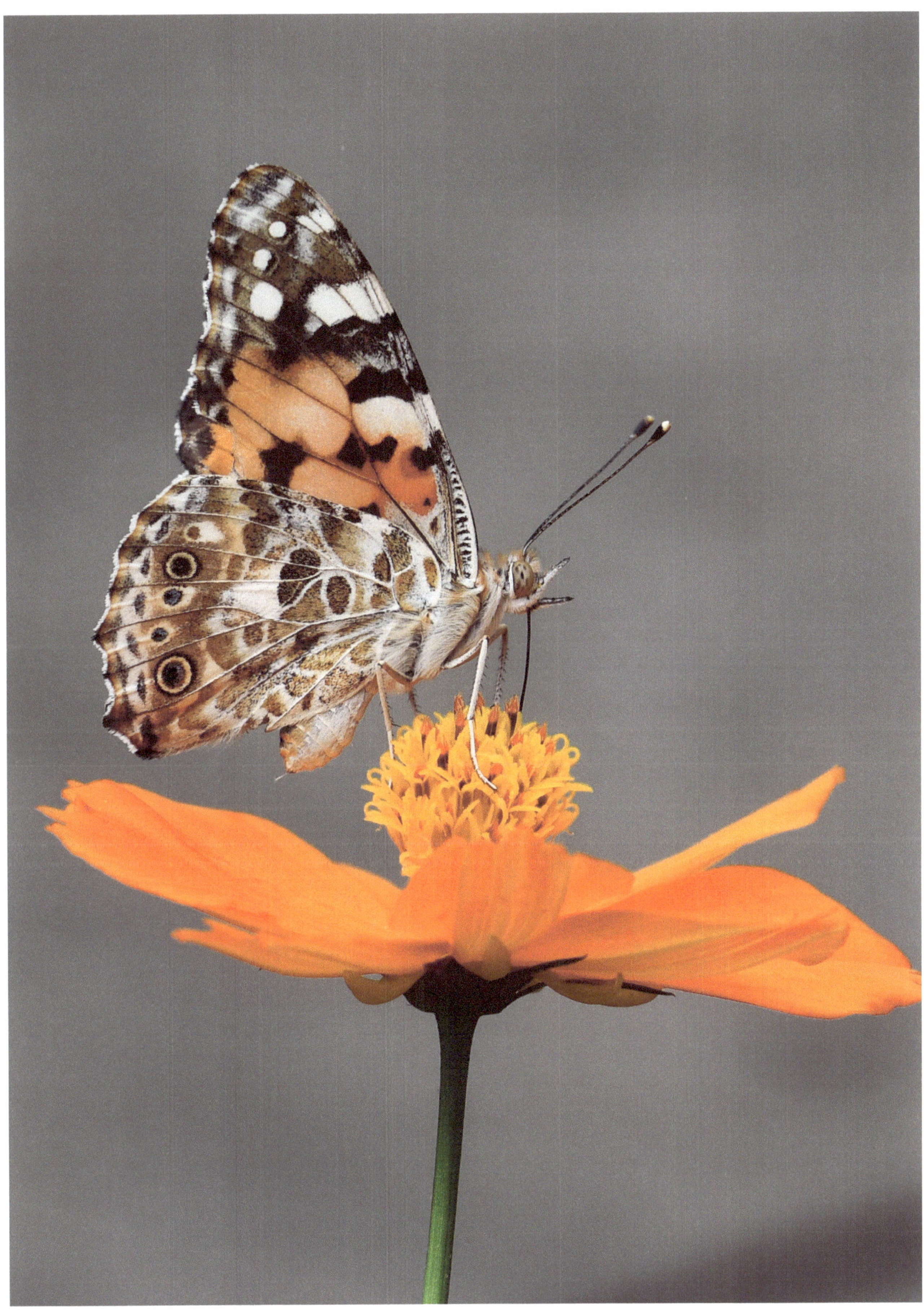

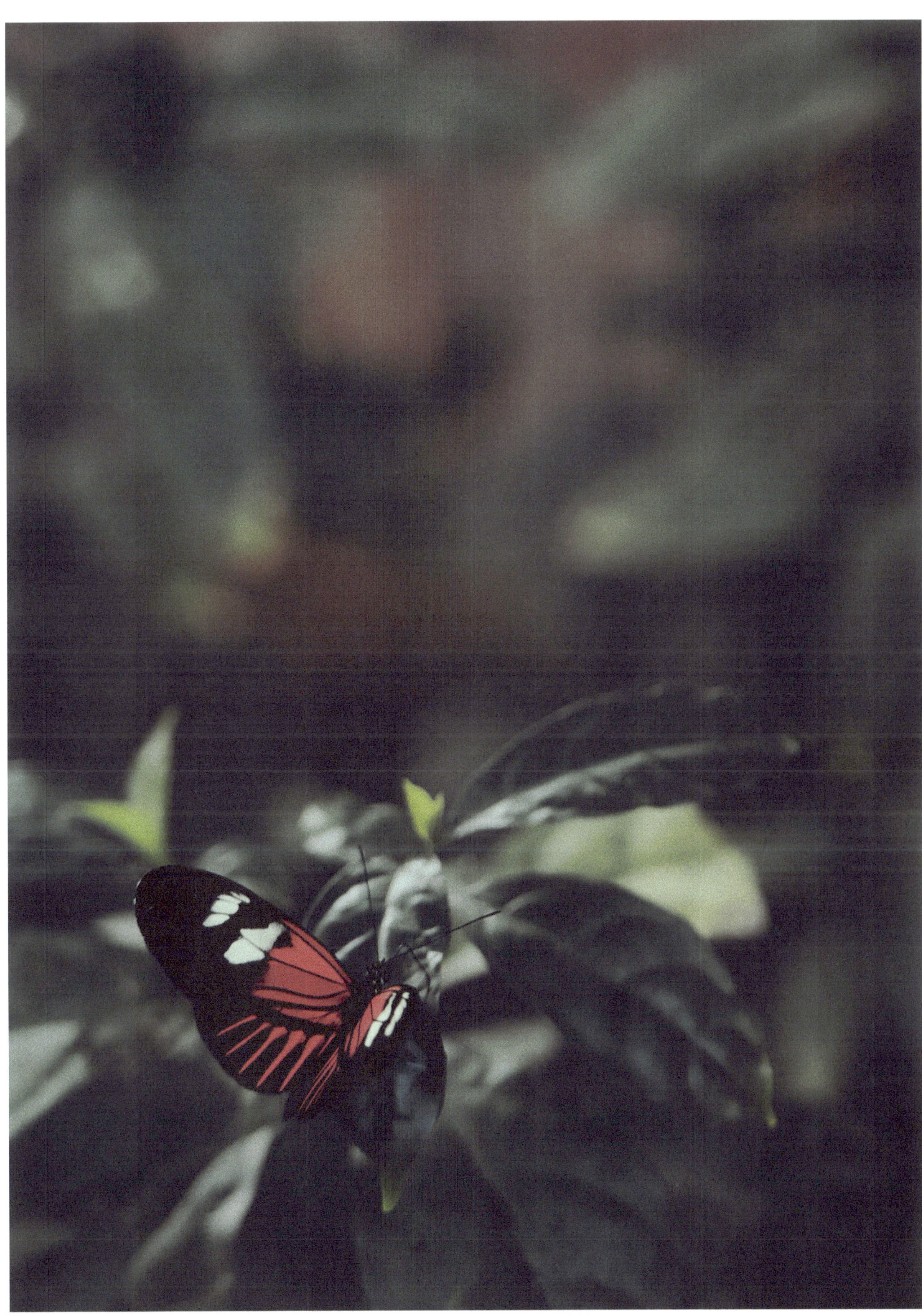

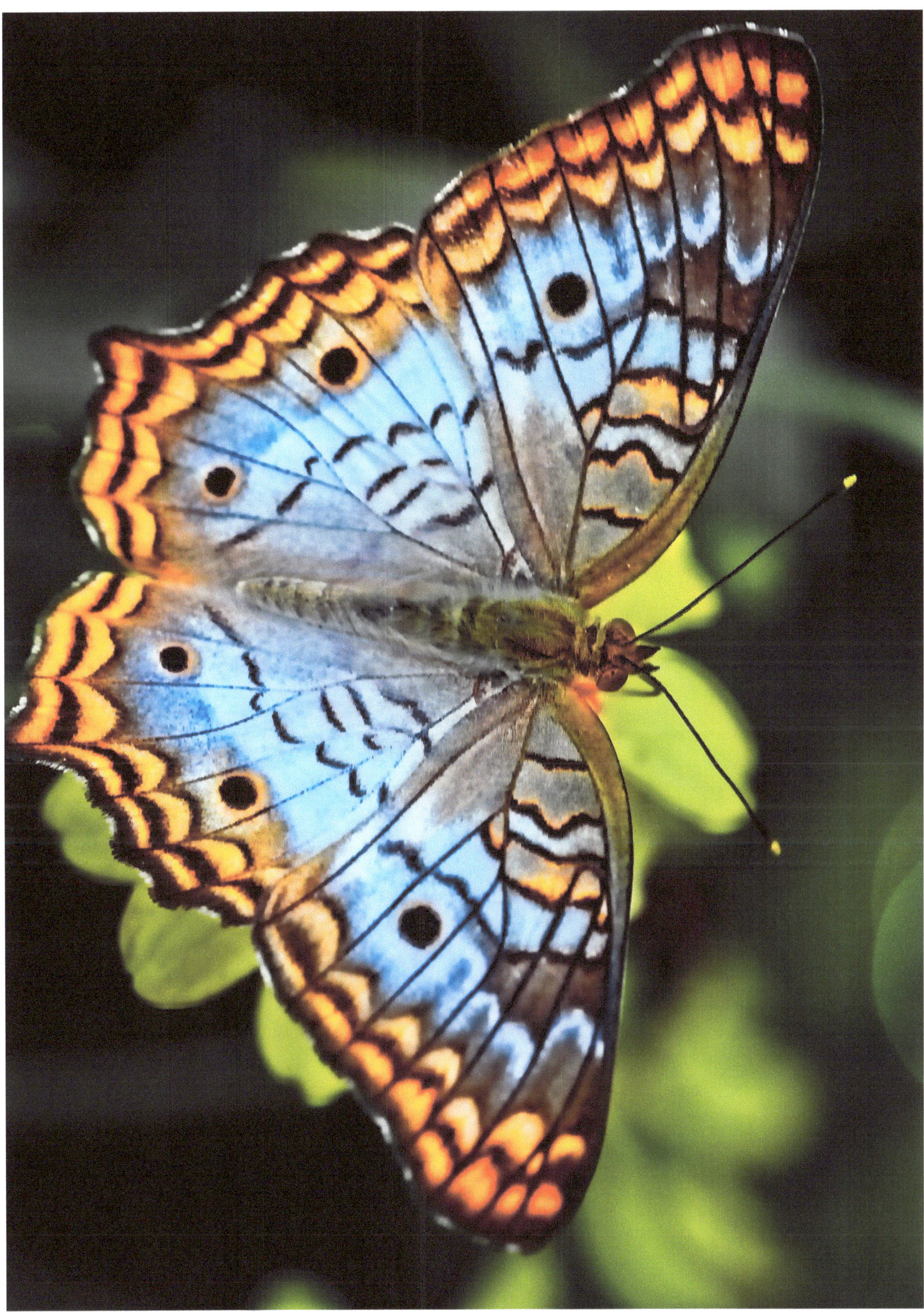

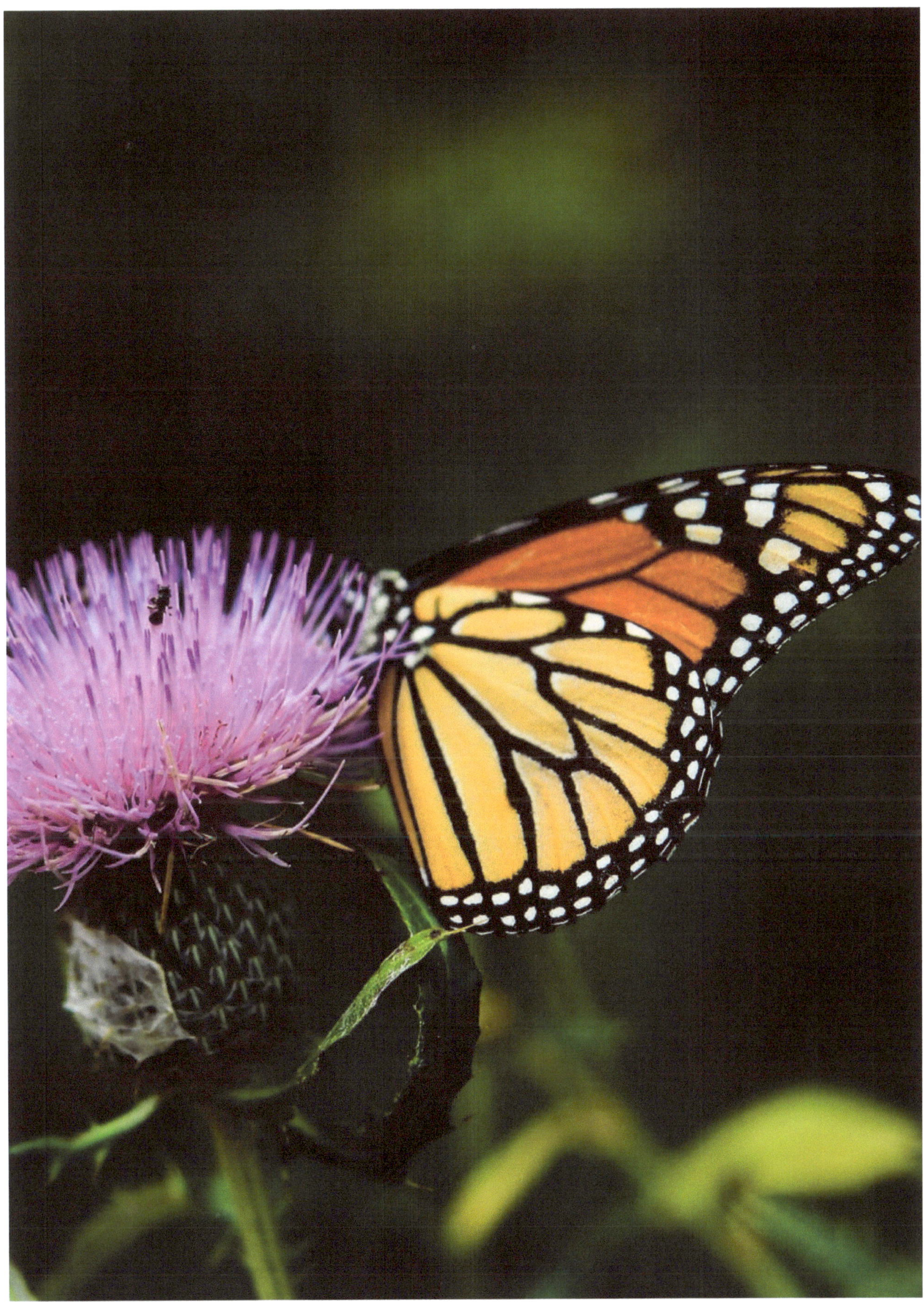

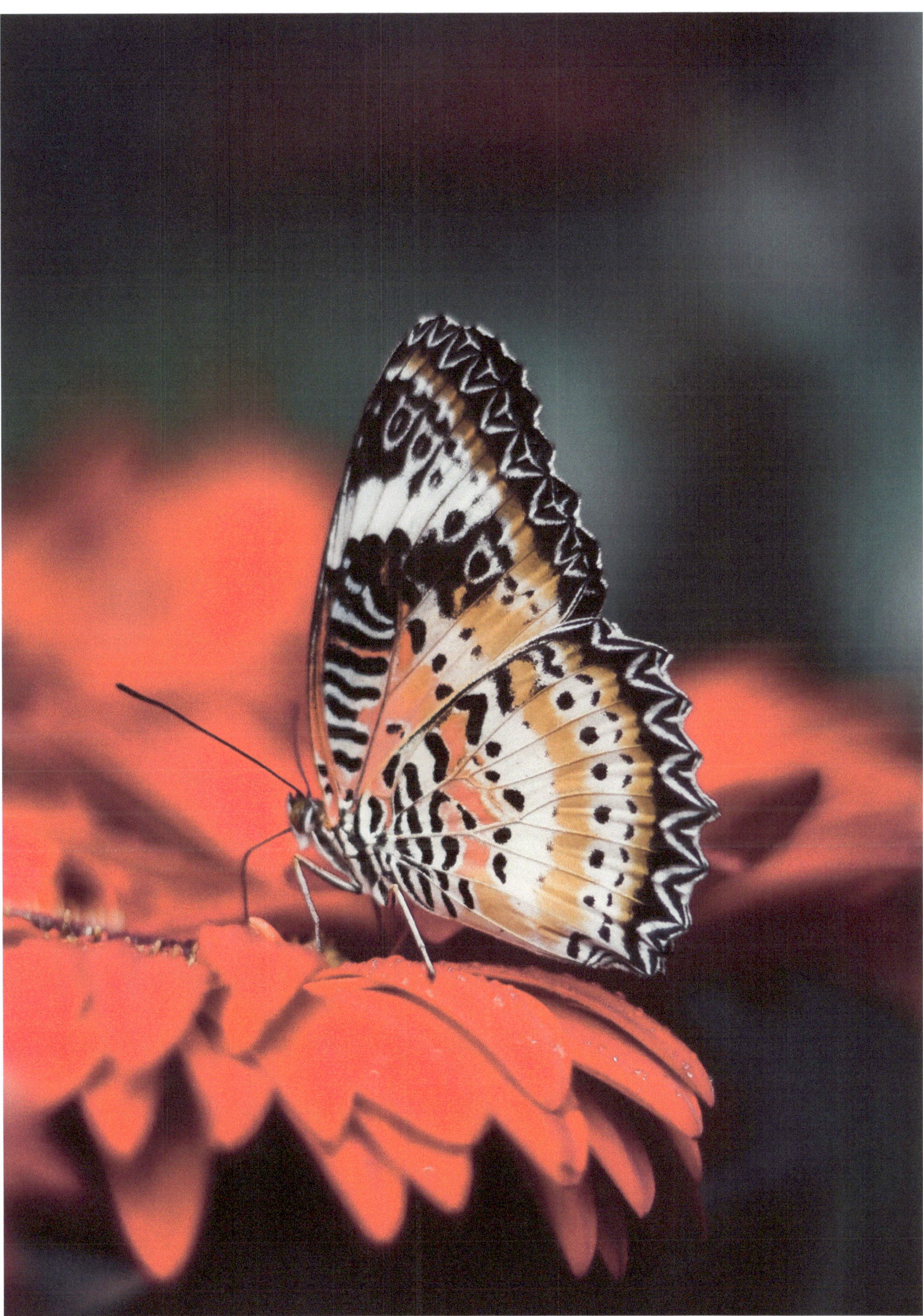

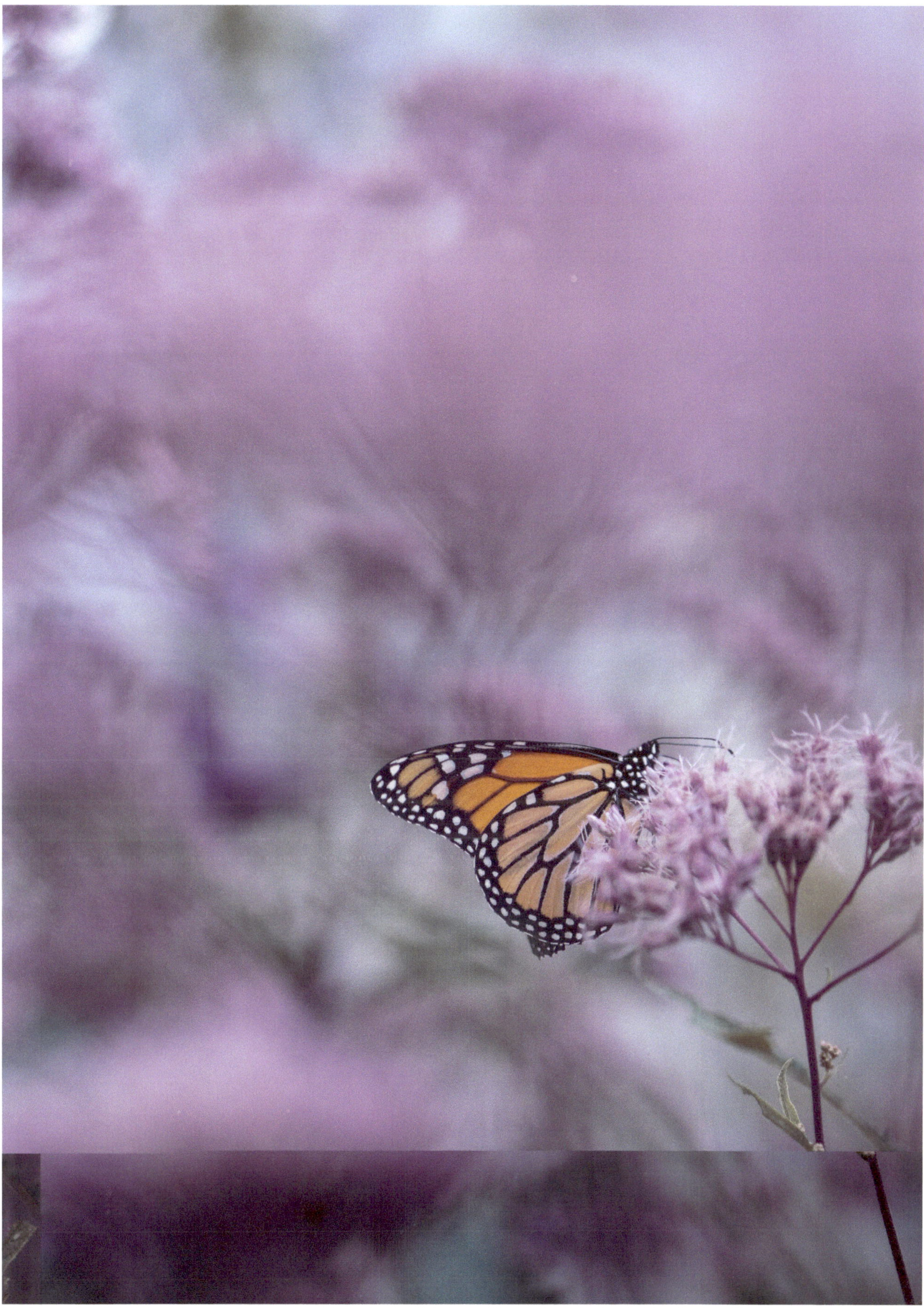

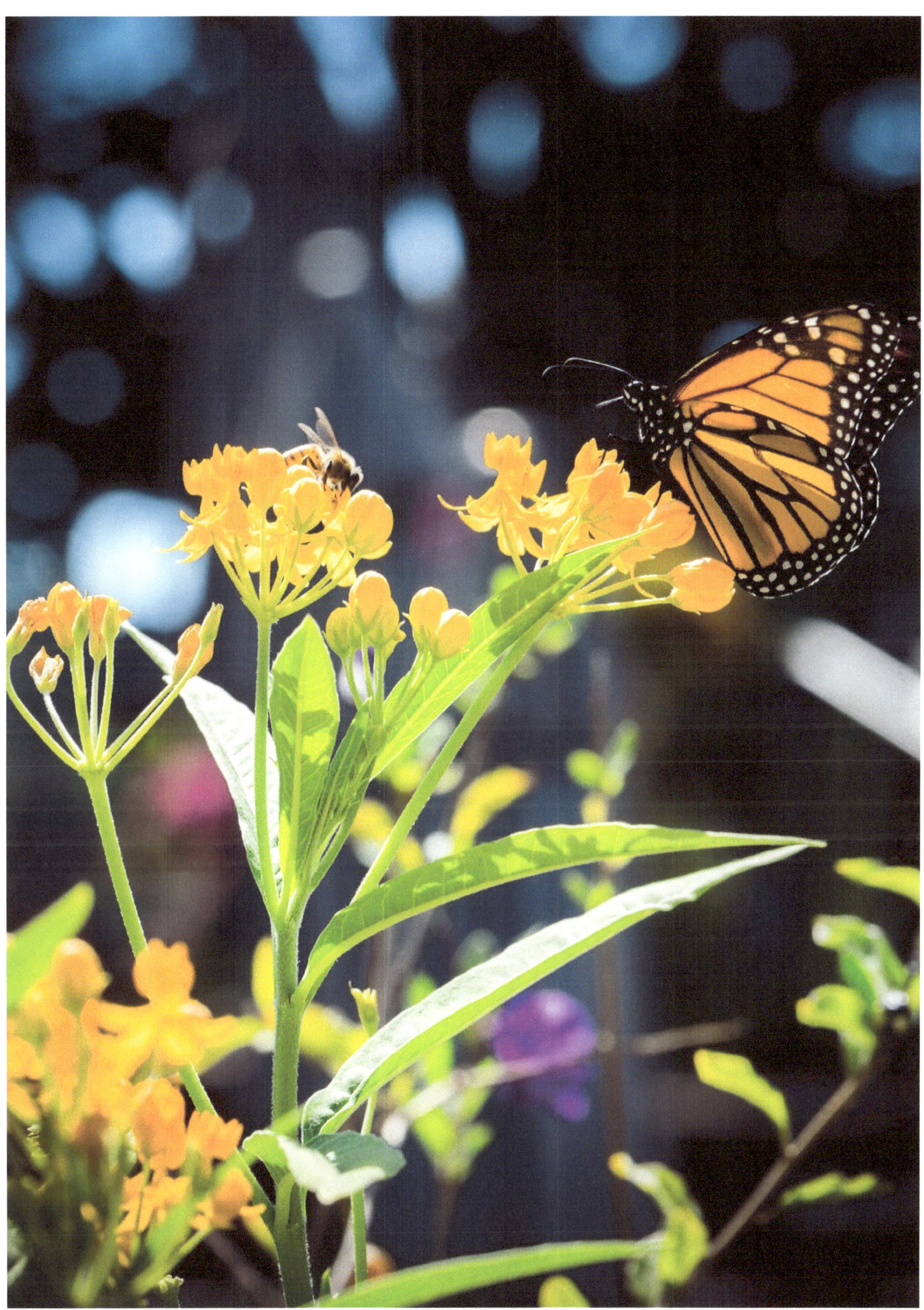

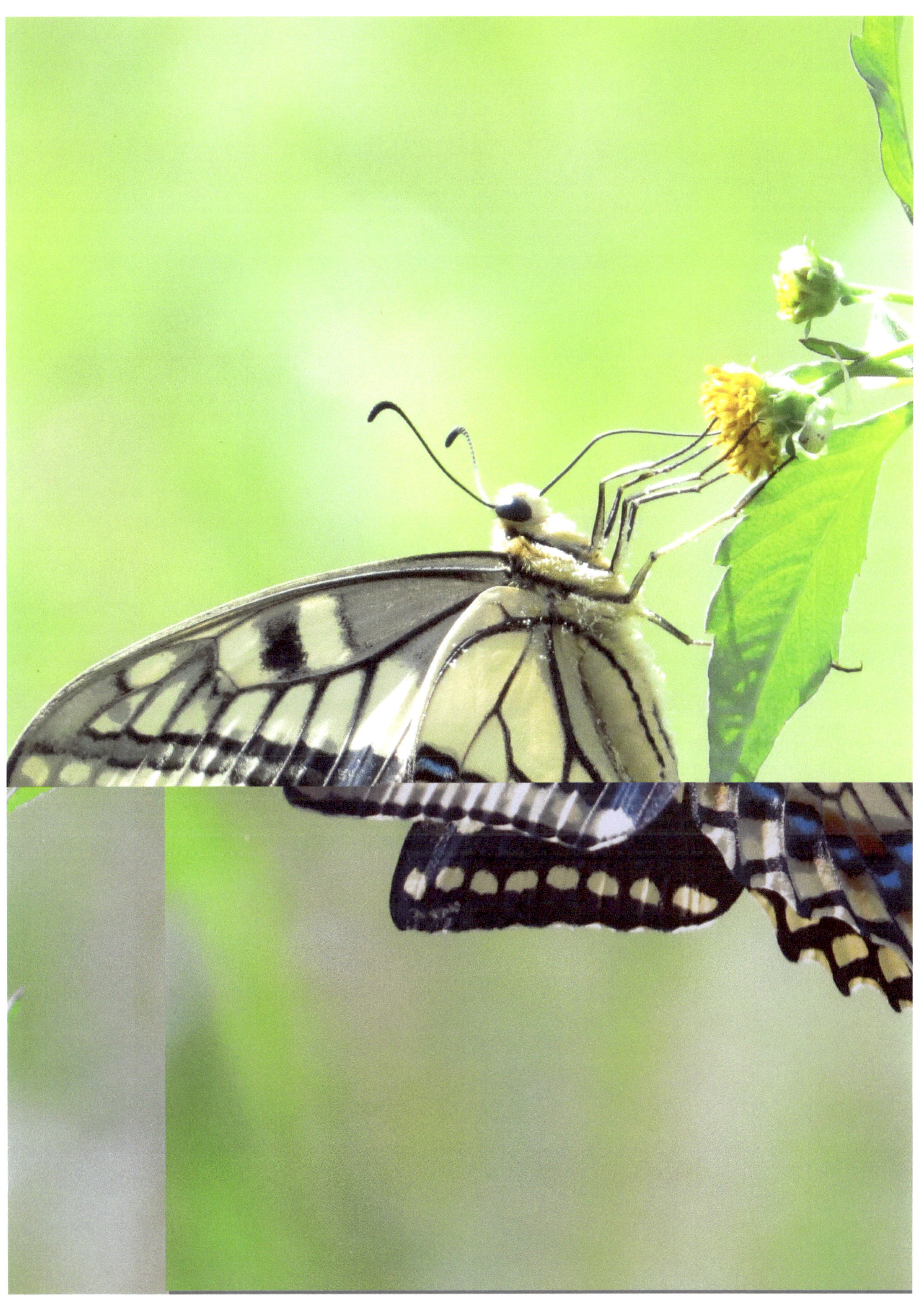

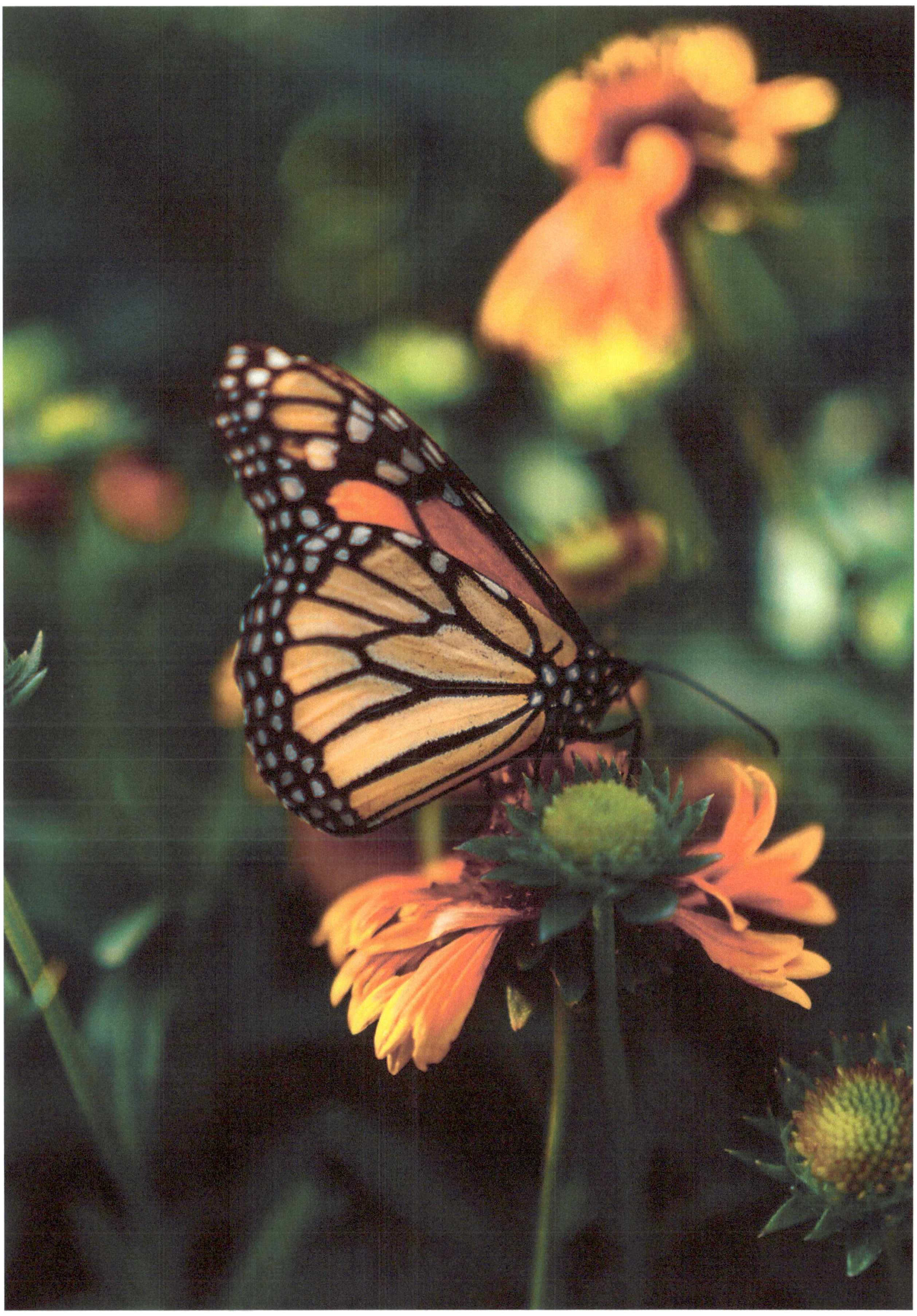

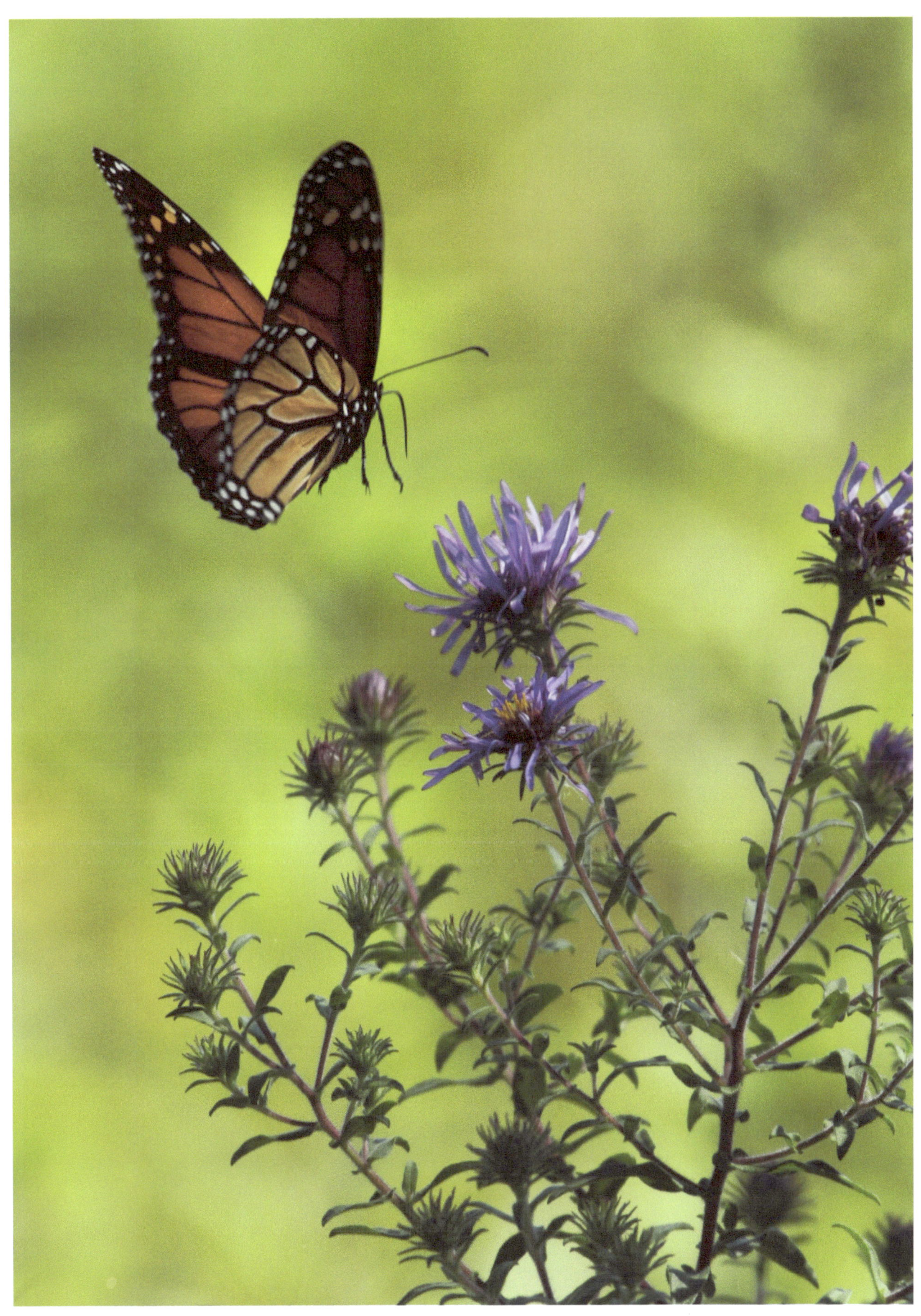

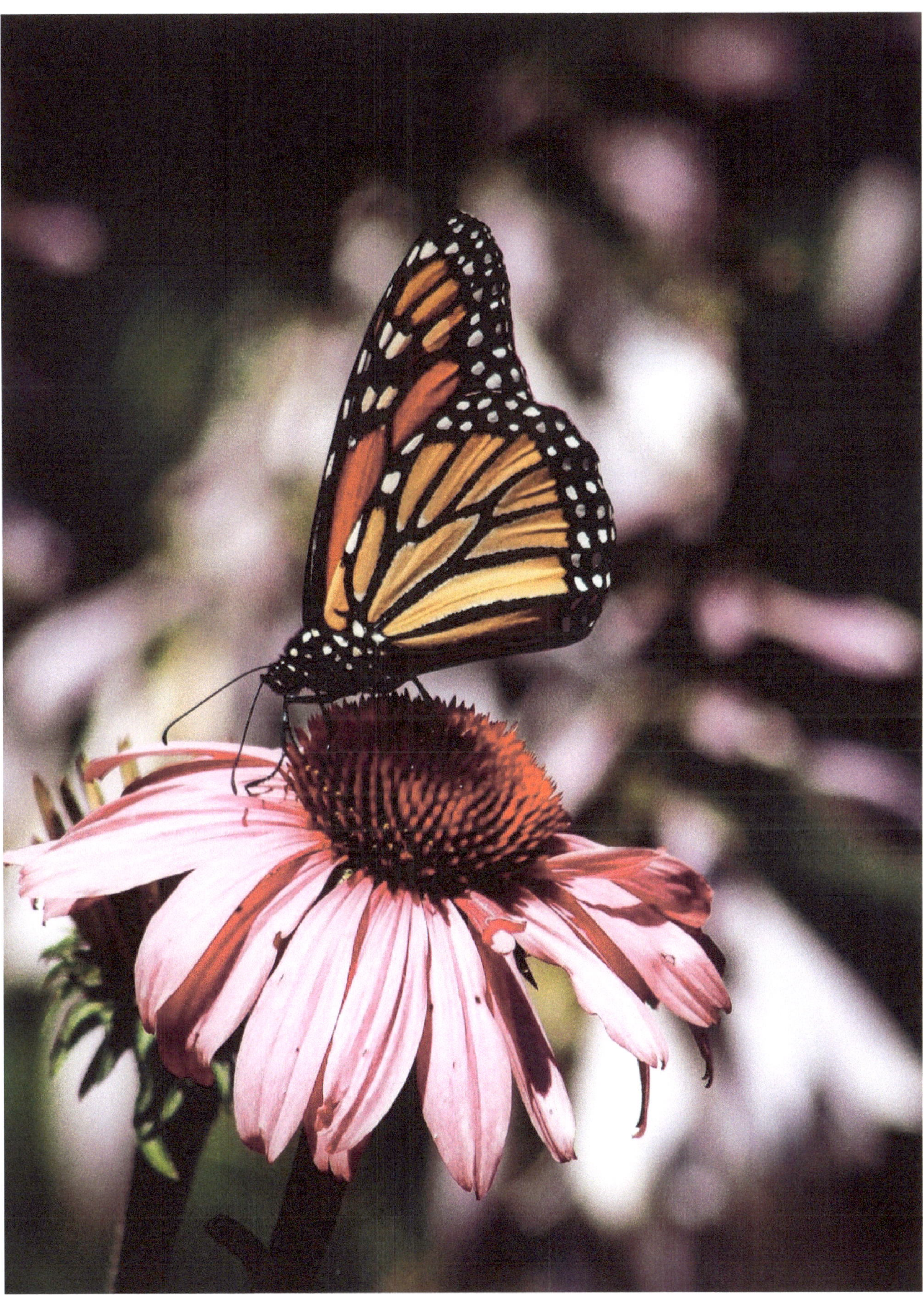

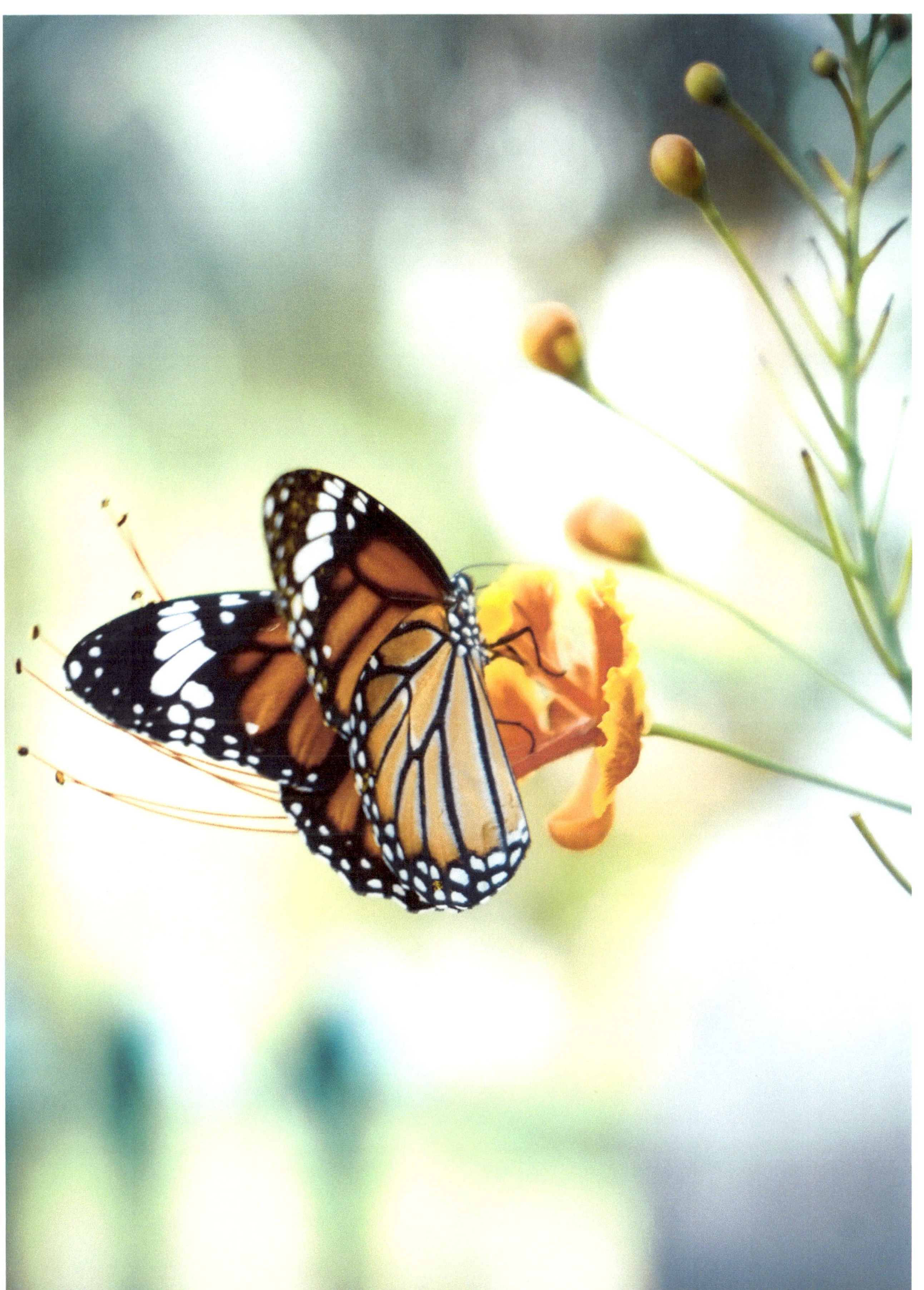